Introduction

In my experience, one does not have to go through massive life changing steps in order to better themselves. If you are willing to evaluate your goals, make small adjustments AND stick to them, then success can be achieved with minimal effort. As with anything, the bigger the changes you are willing to make, the bigger the results become. This book is designed to show you how to get started on the path to living the life of your dreams. I will show you how to take small incremental steps that average people can work into their lives to drive exponential growth.

This book is not a get rich quick scheme that promises overnight success. You will not go from overweight and on the couch to running a marathon in 3 months; or from out of work and broke to a multi-millionaire in 30 days. If you are looking for the easy way out, this is certainly not it. However, if you're looking for a way to drastically improve your situation in a timely manner and on your terms, then this is definitely for you.

I have read all of the recommended books on business and success and have taken away many great nuggets of information that I have implemented into my own life. However, I am not in a stage where I can quit my job and focus 18 hours per day on my passion; I have a family and responsibilities. It is great to be consumed in your goals and have a singular focus, but I can't just quit my job and spend every waking second chasing my dreams. My kids like to eat and my mortgage company likes getting paid. So, I wrote this book as a guide for those hard-working folks who have outside accountabilities but are still looking to better themselves.

I recommend you read one chapter per day of this book. Each day is designed to build on the next. Plus, reading is a great way to start your morning. I know, some of you are thinking about how crazy and hectic your mornings are and you couldn't possibly squeeze one more thing (especially reading) into it; don't worry, we'll go over tips to help you better manage your time. So, read your chapter each morning to find out your life-change for the day and get moving!

It's not a coincidence that this book has 21 steps over 21 days. Stephen Covey, a master in time management, has famously said that it takes 21 days to create a habit. Hopefully, these 21 steps will create new and better habits in you in order to help you live the fulfilling life you desire with however you define success. As you're reading, try implementing the required steps every day for the remainder of the challenge in order to engrain these new habits.

Please keep in mind that this book is meant to be conversational. It's written like I talk, so please don't get caught up in grammar, sentence formation or paragraph structure. Let's just use the next several pages to get to know each other and I will try and impart a few things I've learned in life and business. So, if you're ready to get started, these are the simple steps I have used to make massive changes in my own life. Best of luck on your journey!

Sincerely,

Luke Andrews (Author)

Day 1: Write Out Your Goals

I cannot stress enough how important it is to not only have goals, but to write them down. To me, if it is not written down it is merely a wish or a dream. A written goal has legitimacy and a purpose that dreams just do not. Writing down your goals will help you to remember them in vivid detail, especially when the road gets tougher. Remember, a goal recognizes you are not currently where you want to be, but provides a recognition that you do have the desire and the ability to get there.

Take 5 minutes or 60 minutes and try writing down 3-5 goals that you hope to accomplish in this process. Write down 3-5 goals that you want to achieve in the next year. Finally, write out 3-5 crazy, out-of-this-world goals that you're almost too embarrassed to admit. I'll tell you one of mine: I am not in the entertainment business. I am not an actor, I am not a director, nor do I have talent for either of these things. However, I have a goal to win an Oscar and stand on that stage by the time I'm 45 (10 years). I know it's crazy, but it's on my list…see, it's not so hard. The important thing is to HAVE goals, no matter how "out there" they are. If you do not have a clear view of where you are going, how are you ever going to get there?

If you're still having trouble coming up with your goals, then try answering these questions:

1. What do I want to get out of this book?
2. What vacation would I love to take my family on?
3. How much money do I want to make?

If the above questions don't get you where you feel like you need to be, it's ok to start a little broader. For example, "What does a better me look like?"

Now that your goals have been articulated AND written down, spend the day thinking about them. Make sure they are important to you and where you ultimately want to go. From personal experience, it will be extremely difficult to achieve a goal that has little to no true meaning to you.

Have an awesome day and I'll talk to you tomorrow!

Day 2: Make Your Bed

Before you leave the house this morning, make your bed. I know it seems like a small and trivial task, but I have a feeling it will work wonders for you. It is a task that only requires a few minutes of your time but can help jumpstart your day in ways you have probably never dreamed imaginable. Key benefits include:

- Starting your day with productivity
    - Starting out with something productive will help you maintain that mindset as you face more difficult challenges throughout your day.
- Starting your day with something active
    - Get up, get moving and get the blood flowing to activate the awesomeness coming your way today.

- Starting your day by checking something off your list
    - Completing a task can set off a chain reaction of activities designed at completing more tasks. Start with something small and work your way up to something HUGE!
- Starting your day with a WIN
    - It is always a positive when you start out your day with a goal and then you achieve it; no matter how small that goal may be.

In addition to the many benefits making your bed has on the start of your day, it can be beneficial to the end of your day as well. A made bed is considerably more appealing to crawl into after you've just crushed your day. And, with any luck, the appealing bed you so diligently made earlier this morning will produce a better night's rest to help you move even closer to your goals tomorrow.

Already make your bed every day? Spend time reflecting on how it is a positive in your life that is helping you achieve your goals. I'd be willing to bet, you've never thought about this daily routine as something that will drive you closer to your dream life.

Day 3: Wake Up 15 Minutes Earlier

Today's task will take place at the end of the day. I know to most of us, sleep is a precious resource that we never have enough of. Health experts recommend 6-8 hours per night and that can really be a struggle for many of us with jobs, kids and chores around the house. With that said, having an extra 15 minutes in the morning can help knock out some of those dreaded chores, or at the very least, help to prevent you from rushing around in the morning trying to get out the door. This rush will inevitably kick off your day with a stress-filled anxiety attack. Starting your day in this manner can have halo effects on everything else you do that day and can prevent you from living your best life to the fullest potential.

I am not saying that setting your alarm 15 minutes earlier will not be a challenge; especially at first. This is one piece that will take some getting used to, but I promise, you will adapt and you will thank me later. I think you will find that it will take less time than you think to get your body acclimated and ready to roll on 15 minutes less sleep. If you're still struggling after a few days, there is always the option of going to bed 15 minutes earlier.

Now that you have your alarm set 15 minutes earlier, the hard part starts. You actually have to WAKE UP AND GET OUT OF BED when the alarm goes off. You may need to try tricks like putting your alarm clock across the room so you have to actually get up to turn it off. REMOVE THE SNOOZE. I promise, you'll love it (although maybe not at first ☺).

For me, getting up earlier has had many life-changing benefits. First, I've found that I really enjoy the quietness of my house. There is something very soothing about a dark and quiet house while I have my coffee. Also, it gives me time to do something that maybe I've been putting off. Sometimes, when I'm feeling really ambitious, I'll put on a YouTube video of a beginner's 15 minute yoga routine. I've discovered that it really gets my blood pumping while helping me calm down and relax all at the same time. Finally, as mentioned above, I feel less rushed when I get up a few minutes earlier, which sets the tone for a peaceful, positive and productive day.

So, go for it! Set that alarm! Get up early! And, start your day WINNING! I Cannot wait to talk to you tomorrow.

Day 4: Get Out and Take a Walk

Many health experts recommend at least 10,000 steps per day for a healthy lifestyle. I'm here to tell you that unless you are a server at a busy restaurant or a professional runner, getting 10,000 steps per day is HARD. I struggle to get them in on a daily basis, but when I do, I notice a difference in how I feel and in my energy levels. For me, walking has so many benefits that improve not only my physical health, but also my mental health.

First and foremost, walking gets the blood flowing. Taking a walk is exercise and it is essential for good cardiovascular health. Walking gives me a few minutes to escape and let my mind wander on things of interest to me and not just work or what my family should have for dinner that night. Sometimes, I just walk to clear my head, and getting moving allows me the opportunity to step away from it all, even if for only 15 minutes. In addition, I recommend trying to take your walk outside if at all possible to breathe in the fresh air and soak up some vitamin D.

I know some of you are thinking that you would love to take walks, but you just don't have the time. Maybe you have meetings and conference calls all day and just don't have an extra 15-20 minutes to step away. Trust me I have days like these as well. In this situation, I like to schedule it so that I can take at least one of my calls on the move. I put on my earbuds with the built-in microphone and listen or talk while I walk. I've actually found that some of my best calls have come while I'm out on a walk, as exercise and physical activity have been proven to improve brain function. So, if you don't take the walk for yourself, take it for your company; they'll be glad you did. Get out there and get to stepping!!!

Day 5: Ask Someone for Help

If you are anything like me, then you have a problem admitting that you can't do it all. I really struggle with not having the answers or not being able to handle everything in my life, on my own. I'm the one who helps others, not the other way around. Well, I'm here to tell you two things:

1. No one can do everything on their own and no one is an expert in all things.
2. It's ok to seek help, guidance or advice from someone who is better than you at a task or an area of life.

Take an opportunity today to think of an area where you are not as strong as you would like to be. This could be any skill, including time management, money management, sales, writing, spreadsheets or something simple like doing a cart wheel. Find someone who is successful in an area where you could stand to improve and find out what they did to achieve this level of success. Tell them what you admire about them and seek their guidance. You would be surprised how many folks are willing to share their knowledge, especially when you stroke their ego a little.

If I could leave you with one key piece of advice from today's lesson it could be summed up in two words. Be vulnerable. It's ok to put yourself out there and admit you have weaknesses; because we all do. Weaknesses do not make you weak, but not admitting them will. Putting yourself out there and being vulnerable can be a key driver to success. It makes us uncomfortable, and stretches our boundaries, and ultimately teaches us something new.

Having trouble getting the conversation started? Try these icebreakers...

- "Hey there, can I get your advice on something?"
- "Can I pick your brain for a minute?"
- "Would you mind to help me out with...?"
- "I've noticed you are amazing at _____. Do you have 30 minutes to show me a few tricks?"
- "I would love to be as good as you at _____. What's your secret?"

These are easy, to the point and difficult to say "no" to. Try it; the results will be phenomenal!

Day 6: Offer to Help Someone Else

Yesterday we learned the importance of being vulnerable and asking for help in an area where you are not as strong as you would like to be. Now that you have seen firsthand the benefits of receiving help, it's time to return the favor. What are you really good at? Where have you noticed someone else struggling? Where can your talents be a benefit to someone else?

Today is an important task in a couple of different ways. First, you get a chance to put humility to the side and think about/put out there what you are really phenomenal at. It is just as important to celebrate our strengths as it is to work on our weaknesses. Next, we all deepen our level of mastery at a certain skill by teaching to others. Finally, it's just a good thing to do. It feels great for the person you are helping and it feels great for you. We all like to be the hero every now and then, and this is your chance. Go out and change someone else's life. You never know, you might change your own in the process.

Having trouble starting the conversation without sounding arrogant OR making the other person feel inept? Try these conversation starters:

1. "Hey, I see you're working on a slide show presentation. I learned a few new tricks that have really improved the look of my slide decks and drastically sped up the time it took to complete. You may already know about them, but would you like me to show you?"
2. "I remember you saying you were having trouble with _____. I'm actually pretty good at that. If you'd like, I'd be more than happy to sit down and walk you through a few of the things I have learned."

3. "Would you be interested in comparing notes on _____? Maybe we could learn a thing or two from each other."

Day 7: Wake Up 15 Minutes Earlier

Yes, it's that time again! Set your alarm for 15 minutes earlier and actually get out of bed. Force yourself to stand up and get moving. Even if it's just from the bed to the couch with a hot cup of coffee, it's important to get up and start your day. Have a glass of nice cold water to help wake you up. The health benefits are an added bonus to removing that sleepy feeling.

I believe that you truly saw the benefits to the last time we did this exercise on Day 3. You've already given yourself 15 extra minutes each day; think how beneficial it will be to now have 30! Maybe now you can squeeze in that workout you've been saying you don't have time for. Or, maybe starting that book you've always wanted to write (how do you think I got started doing this? ☺). The first few days may be tough and you may only use that time to wake up. However, after a while, you'll be up and ready to roll and starting to cross things off your list within a few minutes of opening your eyes. If you're still struggling after a week, try going to bed a few minutes earlier instead of binge watching "just one more episode."

And, don't worry, we're not going to be repeating this chapter over and over...I know you need your beauty sleep. I'm just trying to give you a few extra minutes to be productive in your day and live the best life you can!

Day 8: Affirmations & Visualizations

Have you ever heard the saying "you attract what you think about"? I'm a firm believer that you subconsciously gravitate toward outcomes that you think about on a regular basis. This is why I try to stay focused on the positive by saying it out loud and visualizing my desired outcome. Each and every morning I visualize my day and talk to myself about what success looks like over the next 24 hours. I have found it to be extremely successful in both shifting my mindset and helping me achieve more than I normally would.

Today's exercise involves spending 2-3 minutes verbalizing what you ARE going to accomplish today. It may be only one task or it may involve several feats you need to tackle. These do not necessarily have to be standard to-do list items such as:

- I will complete this report
- I will follow back up with X client
- Etc.

These may be affirmations of how you are going to act or how you are going to respond in certain situations or how many sales you plan to make. The important thing to remember with this task is to make it personal for you. You are far more likely to succeed if you are able to internalize these affirmations by knowing how important they are to you and the one's closest to you in your life. In the beginning, you can ease into this process. I encourage you to not make the affirmations too lofty at first; try it out for a day or two, see that it works and then let your mind run free. Out of all of the activities laid out in this book, this is the one that has given me the largest boost in my personal and my professional life.

If you are having a difficult time getting started and figuring out what to affirm, try answering the following questions until you develop a few of your own:

- What are you committed to doing today?
- What would make this day an amazing success?
- What is one task that you have been putting off that you know will make an enormous difference in your life?
- Do you have a big meeting today? What would make that meeting a success for you?

For myself, I utilize affirmations that affect me both personally and professionally. Each day I repeat the same affirmations. I always add something additional in for a meeting or task I need to complete, but the core is always the same. Feel free to borrow mine while you are working on your own.

I will win every meeting today. I will win every interaction today. I will take a breath before I speak. People will listen to me and take my suggestions because they will be well thought out and well-articulated. People will know that I have their best interest at heart and will therefore follow me. I will be an amazing father and husband because that is what my family deserves. I will be productive and positive. I will use calm speech. I am in control and I WILL WIN!

After I verbalize (out loud) my affirmations for the day, I visualize myself conducting a meeting or interacting with a colleague or a family member. I see myself controlling the situation and winning. I do this to attract those positive outcomes that I so desperately desire.

Again, if you are having trouble finding time to fit in a new exercise, you can use the extra 15 minutes you've been given from waking up earlier each day. Good luck and enjoy the affirmation and visualization exercise. I'll look forward to talking to you tomorrow!

Day 9:   Exercise for 10 Minutes

There are numerous benefits to exercise and it is something that should be done each and every day. I am not saying that you should do the same exercises each day, but you should be doing something physical. You want to switch it up to ensure that you are not getting bored and also that you are not working the same muscles over and over preventing them from properly recovering. I am not saying there is a need to go from no exercise at all to a personal trainer overnight. I am merely asking that you start with a minimum of 10 minutes of physical activity and work it into your day.

Exercise offers numerous benefits to your overall health and life. Some of these benefits include:

- Increased energy for any number of activities

- Increased stamina to get you through the day
- You look better
- You feel better
- Your clothes fit better
- You gain self-confidence from all of the above
    - Increased self-confidence can provide a snowball effect to all of the other benefits listed

Perhaps you're looking at your daily routine and thinking, "I already exercise". Well, in that case, add 10 minutes to whatever it is that you are already doing. For instance, you can add a cardio cool down to your existing routine. Or, maybe you can add additional stretching or yoga. Really, anything physical is a good thing for your body, your mind, your life and ultimately your success.

If you are struggling thinking about where to start, try doing any of the following for 10 minutes throughout your day:

- Walk briskly for 10 minutes
- Jog for 10 minutes
- Do 1o minutes of jumping jacks and only rest as needed
- Do 10 minutes of planks with breaks only as needed
- Try doing a beginners yoga video for 10 minutes (these can be found in numerous places on the internet)
- 10 minutes of push-ups
- Do something
- Do anything
- Just be ACTIVE!!!

Day 10: Say "Yes" to Something

Today, for your success-building exercise, I would like for you to say "yes" to something. In my experience, I have found that it is very difficult for folks to step outside of their comfort zone; especially those who are right on the cusp of major success. I've been there. We, as a group, tend to continue to excel in what we do best and refuse to show the world an aspect of our lives where we may not be as good as we feel like we should be. Today, this all changes.

I want you to stretch and make yourself uncomfortable. Today we will say "yes" to something that we previously would not have done. Maybe it is taking on a new project at work or doing a new out of work activity or trying a new game with our kids. The main point is to grow, stretch and be uncomfortable to the point that we realize that there is nothing to fear and we may actually find something new we really enjoy. Think about a food that you always thought you hated but never really tried. At some point, we've all been there. And, once we tried that food, we may have found a new favorite.

Today, I'm giving you permission to be bold and to fail. It is perfectly okay to not be the best at something; especially if it is something that we are just trying for the first time. So, get out there, have some fun, and try something new! Talk to you tomorrow!

Day 11: Say "No" to Something

The word "no" may only be two letters, but it is an extremely big word. It can be very empowering to say "no" to something that someone expected (or maybe you even expected) you to say "yes" to. Yesterday we learned how great it felt to say "yes". Today we learn how important it is to say "no".

As people (even you high achievers) we cannot do everything. For some of us, we had to set our alarms 30 minutes earlier just to get a few additional small things done each day. So, that is why it is very important for us to learn to say "no" and make others aware that our time is extremely valuable and we are only willing to spend it on very important tasks. It is said that time is the only resource that we cannot get back. You can always make more money, but once time has passed, it is gone forever. So, do not waste it doing something you do not want to do or on something that will not enrich the lives of those you love the most.

You may find through this exercise that it is hard to say "no" to some people in our lives. They may be bosses, co-workers or loved ones and you feel as if they depend on you to say "yes" to each and every request they make. The truth is, you are in control of your life and time and you get to decide how you spend it. Do not be afraid to just say "no".

This can be a difficult exercise at first. It involves confrontation and many are either not good at confrontation or just flat out don't like it. A great lesson here is that a little confrontation is not only a good thing, but it can be extremely beneficial on your journey to success. It is important to see that confrontation is not going to kill you or kill the person you are saying "no" to. But, it will help you to *WIN* your interactions throughout the day. It is key for you AND anyone else you deal with to know that YOU are in control of what you do and ultimately what happens to you.

Remember, like the old slogan from the '80's and '90's, "Just Say No". Talk to everyone tomorrow and best of luck saying "NO"!

Day 12: Track All of Your Food

Today's activity involves writing down everything that goes into your body. I would like for you to keep a food journal that tracks your food and beverage intake for an entire day. The idea here is to not beat yourself up for the food choices that you're making, but to have an inventory of what you are consuming. Knowledge is power, especially with your food.

We all know that your body needs fuel, but we also know that it needs the right type of fuel. We are operating high performance machines. You probably wouldn't put the lowest grade gas into a Lamborghini, would you? Why do the same to your body? You also wouldn't keep pumping after the tank is full, right? So, no need to keep eating once your body tells you it's had enough.

I feel that most of us (myself definitely included) do not realize how much we are eating in a given day or how often. Snacking, when not controlled, can be a dangerous increase in calories. In addition to how often we are eating, most of us struggle with portion control. The hope is that by keeping a log of food and beverage intake then we can make better choices going forward leading to improved health, energy and stamina. The results are very similar to the benefits outlined in the chapter on exercise.

If you need help tracking, it can be as simple as a piece of paper or as extensive as a notebook purchased strictly for this exercise. Another great option would be an app. There are numerous apps out there that help you track your food and beverage intake and can make it very simple and convenient for you.

The idea here is to make it as simple as possible so that you are able to stick with it.

Oh, and one last thing, DO NOT READ YOUR JOURNAL. We will work on the results tomorrow, but for tonight, only write & track; do not read.

Day 13: Read Your Food Journal

Do you remember how yesterday's task ended? I asked that you track all of your food & beverage consumption for a day but to not read it. This served a very specific purpose. I do not believe that you should read your food journal at the end of the day, right before you go to sleep. I do not feel that spending the evening stressing over your choices from that day will lead to any positive changes. I feel, at least in my experience that one tends to beat their self up reading through what they ate and drank, leading to unnecessary stress and anxiety and ultimately a poor night's sleep.

On the contrary, I feel it can be extremely productive reading the prior day's entry in the morning. For me, reading this in the morning allows me to get into the right mindset for good choices throughout the day…starting with a healthy breakfast. Reading in the morning keeps it at the forefront of your mind and gets you fired up to switch out that sugary cereal for some lightly buttered whole grain toast paired with some fruit. This allows you to satisfy your sweet tooth and chow down on foods that provide essential nutrients AND are more likely to keep you full longer. This will hopefully curb some of the unnecessary snacking and reduce your overall calorie intake helping you get back into those pants you've been keeping tucked away in the corner of your closet ☺

Good luck and go out and crush the day with amazing choices!!!

Day 14: Reach Out and Touch Someone

First of all, let me congratulate you on making it this far into this book. You are officially two-thirds of the way done with our 21 step process and are well on your way to a much better you! Give yourself a hand and take a few minutes today to recognize the progress you have made on this journey and reaffirm your commitment to sticking it out and continuing to improve. Even though these are small, incremental changes within your life, they are certainly not easy. You have taken amazing steps and I am proud of the effort you have put in thus far. Keep it up. You've only got one week to go!

Today's task is one of the most difficult on the journey and definitely the most emotional. Relationships are extremely important in all aspects of our life. In order to be truly fulfilled, it is said that we need to have strong relationships with our family, our friends and our colleagues. Relationships can be difficult to maintain when strenuous outside factors creep in (which they always do). Relationships may be tested for any number of reasons, including:

- Differences of opinion
- Drifting apart due to family or work obligations
- Drifting apart due to physical distance (someone moves away)
- Sometimes you just get so busy that you don't realize how long it has been since you've spoken

For today's task, I want you to reach out to someone in a relationship that you have been neglecting for one reason or another. This could be a parent, a sibling, a former co-worker or an old friend. It definitely will not be easy to take that first step, but I would be willing to bet that they will be extremely glad to hear from you. They WILL understand that it has been a while but you want to reconnect. Remember, they have not reached out to you either, so it is not just on you.

Go ahead and take that first step. You will both be glad you did. You definitely do not want to be in a situation where you wanted to reach out but it was too late. I mentioned earlier in the book that you can always make more money, but time is a resource that you can never get back. I wish you the best of luck on your journey today.

Day 15: Time Swap

First, I would like to take a moment and reflect on yesterday. How was it? Tough? Trying? Insightful? Amazing? It was probably a combination of all of the above, right? I know it was a challenge, but I am extremely proud of you. I am hoping that you are proud of yourself and truly see the value of maintaining and cultivating your relationships.

For today, I want you to trade 15 minutes of screen time for 15 minutes of reading. A quick internet search and you can see that top producers in every field spend an extraordinary amount of time reading. I have seen studies that show that the average CEO reads between 50-60 books per year. You may not be quite at that level yet or have that kind of time, but if you are being honest with yourself, you could probably read a little more than you do.

In today's modern world, we are all glued to our screens a large portion of the day. Whether we are checking e-mails for work or personal use, checking our social media sites, glancing over the latest digital sports articles or just watching some TV to wind down from a tough day. It is good to unplug and unwind and I am asking that you take 15 minutes of that time to read a non-digital copy of something. Feel free to read for pleasure or for personal or professional growth.

Perhaps you could read a magazine article about a quirky hobby you have. Maybe it's a quirky hobby you wish you had time for. If you are interested in model airplanes or scrapbooking or Premier League Soccer, there are plenty of publications you can pick up and peruse. Is there a book that a friend recommended to you 6 months ago and you just have not had the time to pick it up? Maybe you are finally getting around to reading War & Peace. Perhaps it could be a new technique to help you get ahead in your field.

The point here is to just read. There are multiple benefits to actual reading and I think you will find it incredibly relaxing and a way to unplug. Hopefully you will find this exercise beneficial and can find a way to add it into your daily routine.

Day 16: 15 Minutes of Development

Hopefully you enjoyed the break from screen time and benefited from the additional reading. Today, I am asking that you spend 15 minutes on development. This could be personal or professional development. It can and should be very personalized to an area where you feel passionate and where you feel you could improve. There are any number of topics you could research, including:

- How to lose weight
- How to eat healthier
- How to build a better spreadsheet
- How to write a solid business plan
- How to best update your resume
- How to speak a foreign language
- How to do computer coding

- How to start a part-time business from your computer

The point here is to work on **YOU** and find ways to make yourself better. It does not have to be a professional skill to make you more marketable. Just getting better as a person will make you more desirable to potential employers because it makes you more well-rounded. You can read a book about your topic. You could read a journal article or do internet research. It could also be an audio book or podcast that you listen to in your car while you commute (this is my personal favorite). And, yes, you can make this your 15 minute switch from screen time to reading ☺

Day 17: Replace One Unhealthy Snack

For today's task, I want you to take one unhealthy snack and replace it with something nutritious. Perhaps, instead of potato chips, you make the move to carrots and hummus. Or, instead of a candy bar, you reach for an apple. You will be surprised how filling an apple can be. Not to mention, it is full of nutrients and is surprisingly sweet.

Trust me, I have been there. It is incredibly convenient AND delicious to grab that unhealthy snack and bypass the stuff that actually has nutritional value. But, if you can make that switch, you will end up taking in fewer calories while adding in additional nutrients. These small but significantly better choices will lead to a healthier lifestyle, a better fitting wardrobe and a better looking, more productive you. Go out there and eat well and look & feel good! Remember, one good choice leads to another.

Day 18: Let's Reduce the Sugar

You are getting so close; congratulations! Take a moment and celebrate your success today! You have come extremely far and are right on the cusp of completing this program and jumpstarting your new and improved life. Let's finish strong!

Today, we are going to replace one sugary drink with a tall, cool glass of water. Our bodies are made up primarily of water and we need to continuously pump more and more in to replace what we lose in sweat. Your body needs optimal amounts of water to function at max capacity and keep you running strong and smooth all day long. Try and find an area where you can make this essential swap that will offer multiple benefits to your health and to your life.

Do you drink sugary sodas, flavored coffees, iced mochas, even diet sodas loaded with artificial sugars? If so, these are what we are looking to replace. Don't worry, I am not asking you to go cold turkey and give them up all together. Start by replacing just one and work your way up from there.

By making the switch to water you will feel full causing you to eat less. You will feel more hydrated which has benefits for your mental alertness and skin tone. You refrain from the typical crash that comes along with a burst of sugar, helping you to be more productive throughout the day. Plus, you will save the calories, helping you to lose weight and look & feel better. Now, who doesn't want that?

Day 19: Wake Up 15 Minutes Earlier

This is the last time, I swear ☺. Now, I know you have felt the benefits of being up and productive in the morning. You feel less rushed and you are able to get more done. Plus, by the time you get to work, you are already firing on all cylinders and do not have to waste time getting going at the office; you are primed and ready! Do not fight it, just do it!

You have already done this twice throughout this program and I know it has gotten easier the more time that has passed. Now, you will have 45 extra minutes during the day that you did not have when this program started; that is worth the cost of the book all on its own. This extra 45 minutes can help you knock out that development (personal or professional) that we have been working on. This gives you time to make your bed which we started back on Day 2. Plus, admit it, you are not as tired as you thought you would be because you are sleeping better due to the healthier eating, the additional exercise and the made bed.

Do not fight this! Give yourself the time you need to be as productive as you need to be and live the life you know you and your family deserve. Get up, get moving and kick some tail while all of your competitors are still fast asleep dreaming of the life that you are currently living!!!

Day 20: Review Your Goals

Do you remember those goals you wrote out in Chapter 1 on the very first day of reading this book? I want you to dig those back out and re-read them. Really spend some time walking through them and thinking about them. Now, spend a few minutes answering the following questions about those goals:

- Did you achieve any of the goals you set on day 1?
- Were there any goals that you did not achieve but you came really close to achieving?
- How have your goals changed since you started this book?
    - Are your goals more singular, more focused or more broad?
    - Have your priorities and goals shifted in any way?

- Were there some goals that seemed daunting in the beginning but now seem too easy?

As I said in the beginning of this book, it is important to be intensely goal oriented. We do not know how we are going to get to our destination if we do not have a clear path laid out. Not only is it important to have goals, but it is extremely important to periodically check in on our progress and note whether or not we are on the right track. So, continuously review and monitor your goals to not only make necessary adjustments, but also to celebrate our successes. If goals are a way to mark our path, then we must celebrate the milestones along the way.

Congratulations on all of your progress throughout this journey and I hope you continue moving forward in a positive direction. See you

tomorrow for the final day of our 21 day challenge.

Day 21: Set New & Bold Goals

Give yourself a massive pat on the back for making it through this 21 Day exercise! All of these changes were small in nature, but I am hoping that you truly saw massive gains in your life. And, I hope it does not stop here. I hope you continue to put into practice the techniques we went through together to ensure exponential growth in your personal and professional life. On our final day together, I want you to work on new goals.

After yesterday's exercise of reviewing the goals we set on Day 1, I am sure some of you already started working on new goals; or, at least making adjustments to your existing goals. If you are having trouble getting started try breaking your goals up into three categories to coincide with different stages of your life. Look at:

1. Short Term Goals – 1 day to 1 month
2. Medium Term Goals – 1 month to 1 year
3. Long Term Goals – 1 year to 5 years

Having different time tables and different levels of goals will help you dream huge (long term goals), but also have the path to get you there (short and medium term goals). I fully expect those long term goals to be extremely lofty; I know mine are. Get creative with them and have a little fun letting your imagination wander. Earlier in this book, I let you in on one of my outrageously insane goals. I want to win an Oscar in the next 10 years. I have no acting or directing skills. This does not mean I do not have a path or a plan (that is what my short & medium term goals are for), but it is extremely lofty.

If you are just getting started with setting strong goals, you can research and use any number of methods. I like the SMART method of goal setting:

- **S** – Specific
- **M** – Measurable
- **A** – Attainable
- **R** – Relevant
- **T** – Time Sensitive

As you are creating your goals, feel free to reach out to me on social media and let me know how you are doing. I would love to see how your goals have shifted and offer you encouragement on your journey. Best of luck and keep driving forward!

www.ingramcontent.com/pod-product-compliance
Lightning Source LLC
Chambersburg PA
CBHW020930180526
45163CB00007B/2951